Light Up the Sea

by Meish Goldish

illustrated by Darrin Johnston

Harcourt
SCHOOL PUBLISHERS

ISBN 10: 0-15-350330-0
ISBN 13: 978-0-15-350330-6

Ordering Options
ISBN 10: 0-15-349941-9 (Grade 6 ELL Collection)
ISBN 13: 978-0-15-349941-8 (Grade 6 ELL Collection)
ISBN 10: 0-15-357378-3 (package of 5)
ISBN 13: 978-0-15-357378-1 (package of 5)

2 3 4 5 6 7 8 9 10   179   12 11 10 09 08 07

You may see the sun shining on the surface of the sea. However, the light does not penetrate deep into the water. As a result, the deeper parts of the sea are dark. Still, creatures such as fish manage to live there! How do they live in the dark? The answer may surprise you. The fish have their own lights. They are able to glow.

Can some fish really give off light? Yes, they can! Some land animals can also light up. Have you ever seen a firefly? It glows at night.

Animals that glow are called *bioluminescent*. This word means "living light." Only a few land animals are bioluminescent. However, many deep-sea animals have "living lights."

What makes an animal light up? It takes two special chemicals. They are inside the animal's body. The two chemicals mix. Then the animal glows. Few animals have these two chemicals. Not all sea animals have them. That's why some deep-sea animals are special. Let's meet several of them.

Lantern Fish

A lantern fish has the perfect name. A lantern is a kind of lamp. This fish lights up like a lamp!

The lantern fish swims in the deep, murky sea. The fish has tiny spots on its body that light up in the dark. The lantern fish glows when it hunts for food. The lantern fish swims around in the water. Smaller fish see its light. They are drawn to it. Gulp! The lantern fish has its meal!

Lantern fish are rather small creatures. They are only about six inches (15 cm) long. These fish stay in the deep water during the day. At night, they move to shallower water. That's where they hunt for food.

A lantern fish also glows to find a mate. The fish shines in the dark water. Then another lantern fish sees the first fish glowing and is drawn to it. Now the two are a couple!

Anglerfish

A person who fishes is sometimes called an *angler*. Imagine a fish that goes fishing. That's what an anglerfish does! It fishes for its food. How does it do it? With its light, of course!

The anglerfish has a small rod on its face. It looks a bit like a fishing pole. The tip of the rod glows! The anglerfish waves its light near another fish. The other fish comes toward the light. The anglerfish opens its big mouth. The other fish is doomed. It's quickly eaten!

Not all anglerfish have a "fishing pole." Only the females have these special fishing poles. Male and female anglerfish are different in other ways, too. For instance, their sizes are very different. The female may grow to five feet (1.5 m) long. The male is much smaller—only about four inches (10 cm) long.

Does the female use her light to find a mate, too? No, she doesn't. She uses her smell to draw a male anglerfish to her. The male becomes attached to the female. The two of them literally form a life-long bond! They are mates for life!

Squid

A squid is a deep-sea animal, but it is not a fish. It has no bones. Its body is very soft and has ten arms. The squid can light up in dark waters, too.

A squid uses its light to stay safe. If a squid sees an enemy nearby, the squid makes a cloud of dark ink. The ink has a glow. It surprises the enemy. Then the squid can swim away.

A squid can glow in other ways, too. An enemy swims in the water and looks for the squid's shadow. The squid makes its belly glow. The light fools the enemy. As a result, it can't see the squid.

A squid can even change the color of its light. In warm water, the squid makes a green light. In cold water, it makes a blue light. The color matches the water around it. The enemy doesn't see the squid.

Does a squid need its light? Certainly! Light may be the squid's most important tool.

Jellyfish

When is a fish not a fish? When it's a jellyfish! Don't let the name fool you. A jellyfish is not a fish, yet it is a deep-sea animal.

There are many kinds of jellyfish. Some can light up. They have the gift of glowing. One kind of jellyfish even looks like a lightbulb. Now that's a bright animal!

Jellyfish use their glow to stay safe. They do this in different ways. Some jellyfish make bright flashes of light that scare away the enemy. Other jellyfish make thousands of dotted lights in the water. The lights fool the enemy. It thinks the lights are something else. It doesn't see the jellyfish.

Some jellyfish make a sticky material. This material glows. It sticks to the enemy. Now the enemy glows, too! It draws other enemies to it. The hunter becomes the hunted. The jellyfish is out of danger.

Krill

Krill are tiny deep-sea animals. The smallest are only about 0.5 inches (1.3 cm) long. The largest are about 6 inches (15 cm) long. All of them can light up.

Krill use their lights to eat. Krill hunt at night. They start in the dark, deep part of the sea. They come up to shallower water. They shine their light. It helps them to find food.

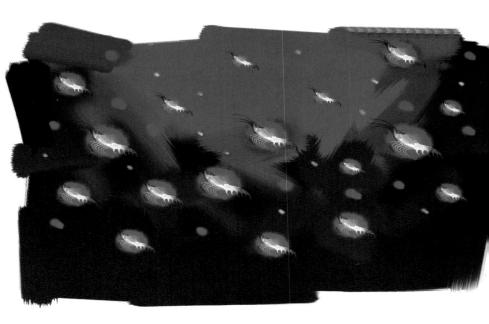

The biggest worry for krill isn't eating. It's being eaten! Krill are quite small. Other sea animals go after the krill. For example, some whales are known to enjoy these tasty critters. Luckily, krill use their light to stay safe. Krill have a plan. Sometimes millions of krill form a group. They swim together in the dark water. The lights make them look like part of the water. Other sea animals are fooled and leave the krill alone. How do krill know when to meet? They use their light to tell other krill to join them!

Now you've learned about some glowing sea creatures. Who would have thought that glowing in the dark could be so useful? At least for a fish!

Scaffolded Language Development

MOCK-DIALOGUE With students, re-read the following passages from page 3 of the book:

How do they live in the dark? The answer may surprise you. The fish have their own lights.
Can some fish really give off light? Yes, they can!

Explain to students that the author is engaging in mock-dialogue. In mock-dialogue, an author or speaker asks questions and then answers them. There are no quotation marks in mock-dialogue.

Have students find other examples of mock-dialogue in the book. Then have them use mock dialogue to explain how to complete a task of their choosing. If necessary, model this exercise for them: *How do you make a salad? First, get your ingredients together. What kind of ingredients? Salads are often made with lettuce and other vegetables.*

 Science

Sea Creatures Have students choose a sea creature from the book and look it up in an encyclopedia or research it on the Internet. Ask students to write five or more interesting facts about the creature. Have students share their information with the group.

School-Home Connection

Glow in the Dark Have students share with family members what they learned about creatures that "glow in the dark." Then have them brainstorm other things they know of that glow in the dark.

Word Count: 1,023